AND

POEMS 1970-2017

AND

POEMS 1970-2017

Michael Mackmin

HAPPENSTANCE

By the same author:

From *There to Here* (pamphlet), HappenStance, 2011
Twenty-Three Poems (pamphlet), HappenStance, 2006
Connemara Shore (pamphlet), Caspar and Rabbit, 1978
The Play of Rainbow, Cape Goliard Press, 1970

ACKNOWLEDGEMENTS:

Thanks to the editors of the following magazines in which poems
have appeared: *Bananas, Eastern Daily Press, Fat Chance, Modern Poetry in
Translation, Other Poetry, Peace News, Poetry London, Seam, Smiths Knoll,
The Forward Book of Poetry 2001, The North, The Poetry Paper, The Rialto,
The SHOp, Transatlantic Review.* Apologies to any editors accidentally
missed from this list.

Some poems also appeared in *The Play of Rainbow* (Cape Goliard, 1970),
Connemara Shore (Caspar and Rabbit, 1978), *Poems* (1980, self-published,
self-suppressed), *Twenty-Three Poems* (HappenStance, 2008),
From There to Here (HappenStance, 2011).

NOTE FOR VISUALLY IMPAIRED READERS:

The book jacket is solid grey with all print in white and centred. The
author's name on the front cover is in lower case about half way down.
Below this the book title ('AND') is in very large caps, beneath which
the subtitle (Poems 1970 - 2017) appears in smaller lower case. There
are no images.

First published in 2017
by HappenStance Press
21 Hatton Green, Glenrothes KY7 4SD
www.happenstancepress.com

ISBN: 978-1-910131-40-4

Printed and bound in the UK
by Ashford Colour Press Ltd

Contents

I do not understand
love. It makes patterns
out of space, of sky, of birds,
and has wings that cover moon and sun,
and is flesh. Only love
is as difficult as love.

—I—

THE WORD

As to why you come to see me Ms
Muse after so long and asking,
of all unlikely things, I get
a stick of seaside rock—pink
and white sweetness, apologising
(you!) for how you'd been *Sorry,*
keeping you at arm's length;
giving, when I kiss, between the
freckles, a palest rose blush.
But it must have the right word

and you standing then, tall on
your long legs, in the doorway
turning a little, looking back
dark pupils, a flicked smile
at the joke it all is, so funny—
I can feel myself falling—
but it must have the right word

and then *Nice but you know you need*
three more lines, an ending, get
down to the seaside, shop for pink rock.

KINDNESS ENCOUNTERS AN ABSENCE OF KINDNESS

In the middle of the night—well, 3 am—and dark.
To begin with the two young people
(her and him) finding, recognition, each the other,
her with red currants, bunches,
that sharp red, hung on her ears;
and him, lanky and diffident, matching
her tallness, the joy unexpected, their hearts
swell, the almost pain of it,
then both saying the three special words.

But later clearing the old man's house
the mad doctor, dead at last, heaps
of dark stuff, woollen mostly, and grey
linen. Also unwieldy and odd things,
the Box Of Tricks (luggage label) leather
or leatherette, the 'tricks' being the clasps
zippers, buttons, all undoable but leading
nowhere: the Bag Never Opened. Boxes too,
postcards, photographs, landscapes, bridges,

some foreign land. Then, curious collages—
the doctor naked gambolling,
bellied, some women too, naturism circa 1930,
and a naked boxing bout. Last, in an
otherwise empty room, three dowdy books,
soft skin covers, printed images,
his stash of shock, torture, a man
nailed to a rock, disembowelled, a mother
running crazy for the starved, the mangled

bones of her child. Impalings, crucifixions,
all ancient foulnesses but photographed—
today, then, or yesterday, meticulous
records: if this then that, if that then
this. And in a cupboard iron implements,
some fixed to the wall, things that have seen
use, tools of the doctor's secret trade.
Last, at the window, *piu, piu, piu,* a small
owl alarmed in the night's obscurity.

MAY

Midnight and the Moon has covered Italy in snow,
Another Little Ice Age on the way. Two
Popes in Rome, a Woman in Berlin,
Justice with a Sword in one hand, a Hatchet in the other.

The Roach's Heir Names himself King of Russia,
Song Birds turn back, the Turtle is heard No More.
The Rules of Butchery are forgotten,
Humankind sickens on Strange Meats.

Scorpions grow Wings, are skilful in the air,
No one can remember the Exact Words of God.
In India the Great Teacher stays silent,
A Scorpion takes him in the Neck.
In the West the Old Queen nods and waves, Nods and Waves.

These are the dreams of my first sleep.
Now I will write of my second sleep.

FOR C.T., WITH THANKS

Like the bones in wings her arms.
And in her eyes
shadow that I cannot touch,
familiar as sister November,
her skin silent as the standing cream,
the kiss inquisitive as roses.
Wake gently, lady; gently wake.
We give ourselves; our fire
is stone, as air
hidden by leaves
and moving into voice.
Dear God, give breath. Life
to life, sings.
Her arms are like the bones in wings.

SALT

1.

Everything, the large darkness of her eyes
the way she ties up her hair at the top of her head,
I was going to say reminds me of you, but no.

At sea the dusk brings out the mast lights,
small coasters lulling along; ashore
a slow flup and thump, grey wave break on sand.

The things you wanted my dear: fame,
special pots for making coffee, the Biba dress,
fresh orange juice in old glass ...

She is like that painter's wife, that
Jacqueline, the blue jeans, the cotton vest,
the strap that dips over her shoulder.

2.

Red light going north: green going south:
coral smudge in the west as sunset breaks,

October, September, seven pm, the corners of her eyes;
she looks at me. Stopped breath.

We had the kitchen cabinet purple painted.
Love in a cottage they said, and meant it

but, of course, not for long. Imagine
the way she ties up her hair.

3.
The way you tied up your hair and a kiss loosed it.
She is not you. And I, this late, still wait
in the cliff top car park, the hot chips wrapped,
the fridge at home full of beer.

4.
The lime tree leaves are yellow now and falling,
as also the fig (the last fruit, the last hornet).
I tell myself I should know, by now,
these images I make: her on the beach today
sea bathing then drying her breasts,
these women whose feet don't touch the ground who
skim about in bare toes, I seduce myself with them.

Her white Fiat in the car park.
She has her hair tied, she shakes undone the blonde bolt of it
salted from bathing.

You, round with child, tilt back your head
as I wash your hair in the sink,
then the rope of it, twisted in a towel to dry.

5.
Time is all at once. I am still being born
still dying, still seeing her untie her yellow hair,
still thinking her hair is salt, it will taste salt.

6.
When will the pain get less? It has got less.
It has? If I speak about, it will it go?
Helping you choose a dress to impress your lover,
watching you dressing to be undressed.

The finger fuck in the car, his little Mini,
I am not over it, any of it, I hold on:
the skin of my teeth is strong.

7.
Yesterday the sea was grey as mercury,
a flat plain, good for walking on;
no horizon, a white sky; the gulls sat in the air.
Today it gleams and rolls, a north east wind,
ice in the air, predatory sea birds, skuas,
chase up and wheel round, high to the east
at last to go south, latitude by latitude,
a circle of black wings. Forgiveness seems
absent from my bones. It is just a word.
Pain I feel, love I feel, but this is not in there.

8.
The whip well aimed might lash
again, again, go deep; bare viscera, bone
well aimed, be one broad line. Again

again: also the vine leaves now are yellow
the bloom on grapes like salt, salt the grey dust
on the cliff top grass, salt on the car's bodywork
and glass—corrosive and preservative.

Nothing here helps: same old story;
dog barking at storm light.

She has taken her pig for a walk,
she won't be long.

He loves me is the line.

9.
Winter. The bay is iced over, holds the ship.
She, warm still from love and bare, sits
while he paints. She is knitting a red cap
a red cloak for the baby. He thinks
she is naked for him, for his gaze,
but David is somewhere with his telescope.
A free spirit, scantily responsible;
her feet are clear off the ground;
she sits naked in his lap.

10.

Where is the love of my life? Friday, low tide
sea like blue oil, silent. *Tide's on the turn*
Dad would say, trying to lock out terror,
not a breath of wind, not a breath.

I hunt along the beach for jewel stones,
agates, cornelian; aware, two years back
the sea rolled down this pebble wall,
rolled easily over the grazing land
and on up to the village doors. The salt
is in the land, the grass brittle and poor.

11.

So earnest, so sincere in their adultery,
keen to explain, be sure I understood,
consulting the Ching, the Tarot,
such nice people, such sophists.

The splinter festers, boils up in pus.
I want to be free, I am on my knees,
Lord, banging the pin back in my heart.

After the years of therapy
I still rage on.
Best friend stole my woman is
a good old Country song.

TOM GRIX IS DEAD

Tom Grix is dead and his meadow sold, the man who
so soft spoken that the parish meetings strained to hear,
walked, as he said he realised, the whole village length
with a woman ghost.

All day my brow has ached with unshed tears.
I shed them now.
I saw our house, the russet apple tree is tall at last,
the fruit thick on it, as yet unpicked.

Oh and as I drove towards the Oxnead bridge,
the sun broke silver,
astonished as if the fields were full of angels,
swans and horses, warriors; another
northern winter coming on.

I called to say a new thing, something, I forget what;
your house was empty. Tom Grix is dead
you know, I guess you know.
I have been away, changing my skin again.

We were married, you and I were married, well
that was years ago.
Odd, I grieve now:
I am learning grief.
I saw a flock of larks and
there were plovers standing in the green corn.

It was a woman ghost he saw.
He said he spoke to her and she said nothing but
they walked on and then he realised
and she was gone.

THE TRAP

The heart trap
boxes me: I clump & thump,
I cry my *Yes*,
my anger bruised on walls.

Each atom in the iron
I love: watching
the falling sun.
The rot-choked fields unfold,
ploughed clean at a whisper.

This is all,
this is all,
you crooked broken
muscle &
flattered residence of love.

JANUARY

They say of the light at this hour
it is failing. Pine leaves are
ivy dark, then black. I'm thinking
my cold fingertips, his cock in my mouth,
the ladder to the attic room, the steepled
roof, a mattress on the dipped floor,
us sleeping half in half out of our clothes.

The eleventh hour on a moonless night
and the marriage has not yet failed.
She can still laugh—*He makes me
come*. She teaches him, brings out
his eye for colour and line, is
growing back her hair after
the affair. He peels apples,
dips apple in sugar—sweet
grit. They have all the world's time.

THE BUG THAT CAUSES MADNESS

is a small bug not visible
to the naked eye
it has a great many legs
some say twelve some forty-nine
it is not clear
some say the legs indicate
developmental stages
others say the legs
sign various subspecies

actually they are more
oars than legs
the bug lives in saliva
in the mouths of other bugs
and these bugs are
just inside the anuses
of much larger bugs
but all of them so damn small
you can't see them

you will think you are getting
flu or that last night's fish
was not well chosen
asexual and as I said
possibly polymorphic
the bug in the human liver
goes torpid secretes
enzymes to chitinize
its ectoderm

it is this stuff causes
the trouble Chou
and Chou (1994, p. 12)
suggest jumping
(up and down) to dislodge
the bug they are
being facetious but
in later life Darwin (q.v.)
took to horse riding
this seemed to help

A FIRST MEETING

Pale but not the moon, not that
white firework glitter and spark
in a blue night: pale like her breast
I imagine. Two swans rest on the lake
and beyond is the house with its stone front,
its pillars and pediments. She has cut her hair,
red, dark, the short burn of it here
under the green alders. The waterfall,
the scratching songbirds in the new reeds, sound
muting my voice, her voice, at a first meeting.
And if my hand reached out? Also pale
her fingers describe the flights, different,
of hawk, falcon, the flickering beat of love.

SUSANNAH

Is her face pale, or pale because she has
some skill in pallor? Some unguent, some
bottled moon? Or maybe the white is because
her black of hair, black of eyes, invents
white skin? My eyes are brown—
not so keen as once they were. And that's the why
of all I do is celebrate her round pale face,
her thin wrists stuck out of a dark jacket,
someone I'd once have called a 'girl'
standing, 8 pm, glass in hand,
being looked at in a bar.

THE AURELIAN

The 'i' as she speaks it, is short, soft, as in
'sibling'. *Siberia*, she says, I am from *Siberia*—
a smile, blue jeans, blue eyes—a long journey
to come to be stood in a dented caravan, here
in the Marsham layby, selling asparagus,
'local' fruit, flowers (*You like? You want?*)—pale
skin, pale hair. *Here is small*, she says, thinks,
points to the glebe fields. *My country big.* Also,
*Here small streets, small houses, all small: first
I feel sick, but now I like.*

I catalogue blue butterflies to collect
the colour of her eyes: the upper wings,
Small Blue, Large Blue, Common Blue, the
Chalkhill Blue, Mazarin Blue, the Holly Blue
and, ah yes, you again, Adonis Blue—remember
that softest hair, the vulnerable abdomen,
and then the paler silvers of the underwing,
the wet brush, the painter dips and colours in.

What is your name? at last I ask.
      Name? she says.

NON ANGLI

sed angeli, the two of them here
in Tesco's considering *Hello!* and other
magazines. I'm stopped: she looks:
a blue stare. *I know you, you,*
and this is not the time. Like that
kiss at the top of the stairs
early morning, spring light, a tower
of Crown Imperials. *I love you but*
I have to do this. This what?
This lead-the-dance, this opening
her legs, this kiss goodbye, once,
twice, in the shadows by the door
to the garden where the yew tree leans
eastward. White skin, black cloth
as tear spells *tear* and I am torn.

THE KISS

A kiss. The kiss. Just lips touch, press,
she kissed him, stepped back, looked,
he looked too. She turned, calm,
went out to where her husband sat
on his horse, stuck her hat
on her head, swung up, rode off,
the two of them together, leaving.

He drove home (O she kissed me!) joy
sweat his skin fizzing (Why, she
kissed me!). She told him *We're going,
leaving the country, south, for good.*
Kissed him, dared him. *If you want me,
stop me.* The horse hooves thud
in the pine forest. He let her go
but kept the kiss, fed on it
long after it was fresh.

COLTISHALL RIVER

In her black swimsuit she stands in the boat,
her feet holding the floor of the boat;
she is smiling, she is talking to someone, her hair
(fair, golden, some pale colour) is
beginning to push loose from the pins.
I am watching from the car window;
this is some film, I think—
the green rushes, the black of the boat, the
white of her knees, her skin, the black swimsuit,
the blue sky—and then
I have driven past.

It is not the she or I this
moment in a day, or me desiring (what I desire,
a kiss, to be not
looking from the car window imagining more,
imagining love).
It is, as the saying is,
the end of a perfect day, day on the river; and it is
the sudden illumination, possible
creation of an idea of God—love
imaginable beyond this love, beginning
to push loose from a black swimsuit, not
doing so,
eternally standing holding the floor of the boat
and then—
I have driven past.

From JANE'S SHIPS IN THE NIGHT

a)
Look how
outlining market strategies
(2004—2007) her shoulder
shifts
the chain of shells at her neck;
how the gold
blinks in the candlelight.

b)
Her black eyes widen,
one larger.
She rubs her lids. *Itch,*
she says. She says,
I have contact lenses.
I hold down the whisper
itch, contact; notice
her dark brows, their glistening hairs.

c)
Winter she wears this full
black skirt, red thread in it.
We walk out, go to the hill
snow on the hill

what happens then   after the kiss
black skirt   pale snow
white thighs   dark hair

dew stinging rose in winter.

INISHTURK

Why did we go to the island? Nine miles
across flat ocean, watching the sea ducks:
to those few stone houses,
ledged and propped on rock. Ok
it was beautiful, the sunlight
breaking in the lucid sea to that pale green
cannot escape blue; the geranium
and lily in their cracked pots at the dark
open doorway; sweet turf smoke
laid down by the wind from thick chimneys;
and an island is an island.

Where else would a tall man down from the hill
bid everyone good morning, so safely
at four in the afternoon?
Such a place has frame and courtesy.
We who are not islanders, well—
we are lapped by unreasonable tears
in this outside: washing out from our hair
the sand of that clear shore.

CONNEMARA SHORE

There is in love sadness deeper
than that space falls
beyond the last star. What else
to say? The heart knows it
& will, & will be heard.
This is how things are: explained
as the pull of moons, or to be given any
holy excuse is, yes, matter,
intention, intensity and joy. But still
that is the core, that,
and the expectation of truth—
which is maybe the pale light
reflected from a pale star
in this black nocturnal whispering sea.

—III—

FAMILY LIFE

In the beginning time, when the father
came home from work drunk and full of blood,
the mother hid the babies.

Me, she hid in a carcase. I was sewn
into a dead horse at the back of the house—
which is why, now, I gag opening the cat food tins.

When the hunting failed, he came home
sober, and that was worse. She'd have to leave out
one of the girl babies; there were always plenty of those

and he'd play with it before he ate.
It wasn't a bad life. Occasionally,
after he'd been asleep and laid in the sun

I'd creep out and watch, keeping an eye on his teeth.
He was a beautiful marvel. I remember how he'd
stand and piss, fiercer than a stallion,

splash; splash, splash; splash on the stones. Once
we played at French cricket with a head he'd saved—
some sister of mine. He said, I *was fond of her.*

How did he never find me in the horse?
Well, to begin with he was drunk, but then
there wasn't just the one horse. You've seen

a car wrecker's yard? I'm not saying that was it—
we'd not get lads come by on a Saturday
looking for a left eye for a grey mare—

but there was a lot of dead stock;
and the mother, too, kept at him to put up shelves;
and somewhere, right deep, I know he cared.

AND

I have been faithful to our peculiar love
this more than fifty years, and now
I am leaving you—not for another woman,
nor, as you were sure I would, another man:

but something as simple as a pale painted
wooden house, a verandah, a chair,
and a path between lawns leading
downward to the sea.

Through your grim teeth I hear *Huh*
he is leaving me to go and convalesce, and yes,
you may say as you please, spit whatever,
roll your sad eyes through the ironing steam

and sigh. I am going, I, away and
even though at last I may become
the man you wanted me to be,
I do not mind. You win. I choose

no longer the self murder of our fierce
play, mad potters who pull and twist
and slap each other's clay. These years
moulding my own dereliction

did not, will not, make that change in you
I have these fifty years desired—
and so I go, goodbye, late but not never,
watching the blue gaps in the western weather.

A LEGEND

i.

From the courtyards and gardens the burning herbs,
rosemary, winter savory, and the smell of sheep cooking;
the city is all one stink—smoke, flesh,
fire. She is in her room dressing and
undressing; has already stacked on
a dozen scents, oils, hairsprays, and her
heart shrinks at the inadequacy of clothes.
Suppose he is in a hurry, undresses me
from the waist down, how will this
shirt look with pale legs, etc, etc,
how will I look, do I look, how am I ...?

Distress sweats on her nose, the tears
well in the eye corners. Yesterday she watched
from her high window as the step-sisters
washed intestines, threaded the chopped
insides of the sheep—liver, heart, kidneys—
along the thin skewers, getting the feast
dressed; watched them in their drab clothes,
joking, tugging the gut, carting tubs
of foul water to the vegetable garden.
In panic she looks at her hands—are they
red and swollen, like those of her sisters?

Will they, despite the creams and lotions,
snag in the silk of her lover's shirt?
And the appalling dance is yet to be endured,
the lunatic hurdy-gurdy, the drunken uncles,
fingers oiled with lamb fat, patting her,
brushing against her breasts, thighs;

and the dancers, smelling of cigarettes and fart,
and the wet kisses from school friends,
and the children, mad on sugar and wine,
lurching about, peeing under the table-cloth,
stealing sweets, fruits, cakes, slippers.

ii.
Her social worker says they know she lies,
and cannot not—invents what
you want, what she wants.
A born storyteller, a legend in her own time,
undetectable by the best detectives,
her eyes wide and her blouse a little open
and father, mother, sisters, teachers,
police-women, forget the accusation.
She has seen King John's lost crown and her shoes
were reduced to 50p in Miss Selfridge, and there is
something at the bottom of the garden—
a fairy, a rat, a pumpkin, a dress.

Her social worker says they know she steals,
takes, without noticing, what she wants—
so much so that she calls it *shopping.*
This dress, these black panels of transparency
sewn with seed pearls—she says
a woman saw her looking at it in the shop
and bought it for her; and the lipsticks
must have fallen into her bag. At the ball
the cash she needs for beans she finds
is in her hand. Her social worker says
she could grow out of it, of course, and could
the whole family come to the centre, just to talk.

Her social worker says they know she fucks,
and cannot not: the boys expect it—
how else is she to meet her prince? Her
prince, colder than the burst condom,
the baby she worries she wants,
that prince of the syphilitic, the phthisic,
who once would have taken her in childbirth,
who once would have burnt her—
who now stands in his thin splendour
waiting his time; this time going steady;
the groom to whose compassion, tenderly
she bares all her blood, every cell, every last platelet.

TWO LOVE POEMS

i

Two wild doves have lived about the roofs
some weeks now, making the bricks and slate
their place. Their feathers are pale
and intimate, like skin losing its suntan,
and they have a strange cry,
the half sob of a child.
I take holidays from logic,
making the birds and sky
a pattern place for love: but then
these things have caught me. The doves
hold me as I held the swallow, as I hold
my love. The children's cries break
all subtleties, and yet—

ii

There are always gaps
in certainty. A swallow held
is strange—a thing out of air
becomes beast: it will be flat, then
struggle and burst to be gone.
Its big eyes are brown rivers,
but its wings! stretch them—
they make nonsense of our limbs—
they are their own proud blue,
and would cover the sky.

ALOUETTE

Where is my sister? I believe
someone has taken her.
She was here a minute ago,
her eyes the mirrors to my eyes,
her mouth the mirror to my mouth,
her long thighs, the alleluia
of her breasts. They say she is
gone to America, an ice cream
palace in the sky, four
horsemen riding into a wooden town.
She was here a moment ago,
not even a glass wall between us,
our bodies, our fingertips, touching,
and then, behind the glass, an airless dark.
She was here a minute ago. It is now
three score years and ten since
last I saw my sister.

—IV—

'WHEN WHEAT IS GREEN, WHEN HAWTHORN BUDS APPEAR'

Midsummer Night's Dream, Act I, Scene i

Like the exact smell of a wet horse
hot after a canter: where were
you when the wheat was green?

Like the path edged with lavender and
the white pink *Mrs Sinkins*: where
were you when the hawthorn budded?

Oh we are all fed down tubes
by our mothers and when cut
away left with a knot in the
belly—just to remind us, just
to remind her. Forget-me-not

like the blue of a mountain sky
glimpsed as cloud, swirled open,
closes. Sing of the heart when wheat

is green, being young, abashed
by love, and love, smiling,
stood at a Croydon

bus stop, the budded hawthorn
blistered, opened under
the whitest moon.

Time, that painted galloper, has paced away
two thousand years. Things, still,
are (mostly) made of tears.

THE LIST

The brushes (sable), the water colours,
the pastels, the blocks of paper,
the notebooks, the pencils, sharpened
just so, HB, B, 4H, the even, left
handed pencil sharpener, the italic pens,
the Rotring (TM) pens, designer pens,
the stationery of blocked artistry,
the loose leaf book, the ring-bound book,
books bought in Italy, in Ireland,
in France, the poetry of faint (feint?)
lines, of plain pages, the various and delicious
different weights of paper,
the undrawn, the unpainted, the unwritten
poem, the empty house, the dark
squares of its windows, the track down to it,
the Corsican pine, the five apple trees, the peach
still bearing wet fruit against the south wall,
the almond, the apricot, the black figs, the white
dust of the track, up the hill
the neighbour's thirty-nine hives,
the bees, the loud
buzzards' midday sunlit mew,
the bread on the table, the cracked
dish with the olives (black),
the white jug, the hard red
of the meat, the soft white of the cheese,
the lightning's illumination—death and
tomorrow—my beloved you, so
difficult to love, the grey road
under the grey tyres,
the shock, the sign, the breath
of dead poets which was their all,

our all, held in the air in this valley
where the eagle pauses, its
wings at the edge of a hover
looking for snakes, the locked
church, the roses yet budding
more red, more white, the unexamined life,
the mantis on the stone step,
the closed book, the door
latched with string, the four men
in the sunset bar, the cards in their hands.

THIS POEM EXPLAINS

This poem explains the meaning of life,
especially for our time. I write
as my tutors here advise, of things
I know. They also say to *show not*
tell which I also do. Philosophy
is my hobby poetry my passion
as I'm sure you'll see. In stanza one
'*The Picardy roses are sodden and spattered*
in mud' refers to the First World War
and a popular marching song
then. However, it is a metaphor for all
the beautiful young men dead, donkeys
led by lions, as has been said.
In stanza two, '*The secret diarist*
in her attic lair' refers to Anne
Frank who hid in an attic and
her family. Hitler wanted all Jews
dead and nearly succeeded. Some say
he is misunderstood but I think not.
'*The burning child who runs along the road*'
in stanza three refers to a photo
from the Vietnam war in black and white:
a naked child runs away from the war
and luckily was captured on film—
I explain the pity and terror.
In stanza four, '*Sponsored now*
by Sky and CNN' is an original
idea of mine and Copyright—the idea is
that in our time the media will pay
for wars for people to watch. I hope
you like my poem. I hope you like my poem.

THE COMPOSER

Moving deliberately among bees
at the extreme edge of a universe
is how his music sounds.

Short thick fingers hold a comb;
some wasps leave the plum orchard,
stray into the hairs on his jacket.

Of course we neither hear nor see.
What is joy? said the boy. *There is only
contentment.* I had to disagree.

Without a fierce joy we lack any
raison d'être. She was over at the dresser.
She had a collection of those ceramic

things for raising the crusts of pies,
holding them up, letting the steam out of them—
a sort of trepannation. After all

a pie too has its bones on the outside.
Without a crust-raiser, the pie might
break, hurl its brains at the oven walls.

The father had taken his coffee cup,
gone out with his cloud of satellites.
There seems to be a rule that says

bear with the invisible; look how
the ladder leans into the damson tree.
But I don't think we have time for that.

PASTORAL

A thin man in a blue waistcoat, standing,
his arm about the neck of a chestnut colt.
The colt and the man look towards the bungalow
where a woman bends at a camera, taking the photograph.

The man's thinness, the colt's tall neck, the need,
please God let it come out, for a photograph—
the mare grazing at a distance;
there is something in this,
the man and the colt,
the woman bending with the camera.

All this can die? How can all this die?
A few hens sheltering in the porch,
the cracked pane, the cardigan on a nail,
a sack of fossils on the floor, where falls
the bleaching light, where light falls.

All this can die. One man makes a cradle with his arms;
another fashions his hands into a cup or bowl.
Of the third, a lover of roses, it is said
he believes they have taken his name for a rose.

HOW EASILY

He brings her his flowers. She
finds a vase for them, stem by stem
into the mouth.

*

And these are the blossoms that were refused
when I carried in torn armfuls. *Hawthorn?*
Not in my house, they are unlucky.
Well, now I know they smell of death or—
my nose in the hedge—
the cunt of this young woman who has been eating almonds.

*

How easily the roses (*he was taking care of the roses,*
or the roses were taking care of him); how easily
the roses: the first rose: and all the lines,
inflowing, and still no entrance; how
easily the rose proposes an end to the difficult.

*

Pleasure.

BECAUSE OF FEAR

Because of fear, I always hurried into love
sounds right, apposite; never without someone
to meet off the train, go shopping for—seldom
myself, stuck at *Of course I do.*
'And of course,
I do know what love is,' he says and thinks
of those so awkward 'So how's the sex?' questions.
Brilliant, we're fine (only to find, with someone else
the diamond taking other, deeper, cuts).
However firm it seems, the heart can falter and decline.

And now fear, and asking love to stand and stay
and be beyond all patience, any bargain, any marriage
(those bits of cake, their marzipan, their ice, all
gone to the birds, the printed cards, the cardboard boxes
burned), it is—well—Gabriel preening, Gabriel
with his long toenails
scratching for ticks in his wings. Nothing
on earth like it, an enfolding, an enfolded heart.

—v—

POURED WATER

This is the time of the musk rose,
so pale in the moonlight, and honeysuckle,
and the hang of green plums
thickening on the trees.

In those days I'd trudge home, wood dust
in my hair, in my brows; fingertips
soft from sanding wood, dark
chemicals under my nails

and would put the day's money
weighted by a stone, on the kitchen
shelf, thin paper-fold,
the next day's food.

And one day, let this be said, weary
I came in & she sat me down, took
a lump of soap, a piece of towel,
the chipped enamel bowl, love,

sweet love, dear God, let this be said:
that red-haired woman, now dead, wearing
her neat grey apron, poured water
from a jug, washed my feet.

THE BLUE ROPE

1

The blue rope found on the beach
belongs
with those mid century poems:
here is the blue rope

a fragment

2

& includes my loving the red-haired woman
and the white stones
and the burned fish, stars
in that night sky far in the west—
house lights, street lights
long extinguished

3

a brief innocence: we walked,
the night being warm,
the pale road out of Galway city,
fell down tired, slept in the long grass

4

as there was no way else
to pay the fare,
and the German tourists looked, ach!
old fashioned, askance,
she took the boatman to a quiet beach,
requited him with a fuck

5
hankering after old goddesses
and in with a wild crowd,
drunk, sitting in the laps of god
knows who,
nobody's woman, up for grabs,
and I would love you
ten years, and am still aghast

6
here, she said,
more blue string for you,
how did I find a man
saves pieces of blue string,
stuff the sea spits up?

7
it is the sky in paintings,
the girl holding the child,
that rope

it is her new born eyes
meeting mine, she sees me,
that rope

the dye cannot wash out,
oceans cannot wash it out

DECEMBER, FOR LUCY

Watching where a robin stood
and dipped to pick at little
bits of food where I'd been lumping
up and down, breaking wood

I thought about the goldfinch
that I took and cut
to see the heart, awed
how large it was in such a small—

yet capable for years, the flight,
the song, and yellowest of wings.
And this bird here, fat against
the cold, ticks, whirrs along—

singing is it? Is it singing
makes the heart get strong?

HERE

This is an older landscape, smaller
fields, tufted copses, orchard plots,
and each house has its vegetable piece—
the rows of beans, potatoes, clumps
of darker, large-leaved green where
squashes grow, swell yellow into
orange. At night, moths; in daytime,
bees (from their hive beside a stony
bank) work the flowers, while the ground
is populous with crickets, ants, hoppers,
flies. And in the walnut trees a bird
hides, sings and hides again, unseen,
an unknown bird.

It was some such muck-and-wood-smoke-
scented farm Cincinnatus (remember him?)
quit, came back to, when he'd set
all straight, done his noble ancient Roman bit.

THERE

for Patrick

The distant hills are blue, purple,
dark as a bruise against the sky's
evening eye. From here to there is far—
a trouble, a journey not lightly taken,
things being as they are, the price
of wheat, the bigger field to plough.

So when he, the one traveller, came back, we
expected tales—got them: far other hills,
he said, lay westward, mountainous,
where lightning washes, glares,
and snow is permanent. Those who live
there murmur a *beyond*, but
things being as they are, the price
of wheat, the bigger field to plough,
it's not a journey any recommend.

—VI—

SOME DEATHS

What did the kind lady at the hospice say?
She said *he had a good death*, she said—
her, her with the white Irish face, that
mop, puffed, fly-about-hair, and the fingers,
the long bones there in her fingers, she said.

And the opposite?
Is that a 'Bad Death'? He had 'a bad death'?
No. Be Quiet. *Not a good death*
is the opposite. She'd rather always say *he had*
a good death. And sometimes she has to take you
aside, into the room that's set aside, and sometimes
say it—*It was not A Good Death*—as if, lucky you,
you missed it, it was not a good death, blood and shit
and shit, and blood, we held him down we shut
his mouth
he died.

THWACK! Like a mad daddy with his
swishing stick Death bangs the white light
into you: sudden. Or tricky comes with caress
and cuff, pinch and punch, seduces you with
stroke and kiss, and never, no O never says
This, will
hurt me far more
than it hurts
you. Good. Bad. Death dogs you.
Take the lead off its hook,
walk out into the woods.

A LEAN YEAR

Snow on the sand, snow drifted against
grey waves, that mixture of pallors,
and the boat pulling towards the shore,
grounding and the boy out first running
with the rope to the waiting group,
the women, who haul the craft up the beach.
The weary rowers step out with their oars
and under the thwart a dark bundle.
The stillness as one carrying a lantern
steps forward. It is like some
etching of time past—darkening sky
lamplight on the faces making all there
suddenly young, eyes, mouths, hands,
the thick cloth wrapping against
the wind's ice and disaster's dread.

Lastly the helmsman stepping ashore
lifting a child, a small babe, out of the boat
who wails at the storm, is alone
all that could be saved—the mother,
alive when found, gave up
as they hauled her into the boat.
No jubilation. Another mouth to feed
and this a hungry shore, a lean year.

But the boy, his face turned windward,
begins suddenly—prompted by what strange
thought he never, years after, ever makes out—
begins to sing. Women step to hush him but
the one carrying the lantern says, No, let him sing.
Let his song go up for all of us, let him sing.

MONUMENT

It would have been easier to cure Romeo of loving Juliet than it is to cure
a hypochondriac of loving himself.

    Eric Berne, 'Layman's Guide to Psychiatry'

They say that when you look at anything, rock,
stone, the window-cleaner's eyes, and see
that moment as alone, the last, then no
fear can get you, no consequence can sit blear
beneath the heart and interrupt the breath.

This thin red wine, sour as green plums,
I try to think removes all past and future as I drink,
and fail: it is soon gone, my tongue, curled
down, wets only glass, and—look, our bachelor vicar
goes, in his sensible shoes, whistling walking down the lane.

Anxiety doubles back: I check my mortality's
symptoms, pulse, the dim left eye, breath,
aches in the jaw and leg, meditate and note
I've not gone yet, and yet get no further—alarmed
I might here, this ordinary Sunday evening, dare

employ some image would allow I am content.
(Mist clears, the stone wall runs along the hill line,
the hill named like a dance, Pen y Ghent.) (Some nights
the stars, other nights the dark is like
a slab of monument.)

THE BEAUTIFUL LANDS OF THE MOON

Occasional witches fly in the sky
While the wild and hairy woolly
Man who climbs the ivy onto the roofs
And I, and a woman, and a dog,
And the man who made the film,
Cram into the small triangular box
(With the rickety cracked-up lid)
That takes us off to the moon.

The beautiful lands of the moon,
The purple and green and yellow and grey,
The blue, the red, the umber, the pink,
Where crocuses grow in asparagus fields,
The marshes and mists, and the moors and lakes
Where terrible sleeps and wonderful wakes,
And the stag in the orchard
Tangles his starry horns.

Occasional witches fly in the sky
Where we ride in our shivering box
And look at the lands of the moon;
While the man who made the film
Shyly accepts our applause, and,
Just as Nothing is lost
And All is found,
The chorusing birds
Fall past the roses and into the room
And you and I
Wake again on the plain green ground.

DOLMEN

A thick blue string was tied
across the track, and in the wood
the place itself was fenced with wire,
barbed, more than human height
which in itself had echoes, memories.
A narrow gate of upright angle iron
led us in. The dome stone, grey,
curved like a skull's top
was poised on four thick teeth:
there was a space beneath.
She clambered under while I stood,
watched the aspen leaves.
The sound is different here, she said:
I went under too and heard.

Where once we would have kissed,
stripped, and she'd have slid onto me,
shuddered, & so on, we sat in stillness—
till, spooked by thinking,
(the weight of time—had I locked the car?)
we crawled out of the shadow,
found the wood thick with the black buzz
of flies, walked to where an oriole scolded
high in an oak. What *was* it then?

A shelter for the dead when—
as it may—the sky's skull cracks and falls?
Or one of many things made to catch earth's
breath, and change the shape of sound?

A THREAD

Ann was dusting the apples.
Her daughter was having her
dressings changed, at the same time
wondering was it worth it.
They both wondered that—never
spoke it to the other though.
The bough had broken and Ann
had had to pick the apples,
piled them in bowls about the house,
more than I can ever eat.

The daughter said to her friend, *but
I couldn't, because of the child.*
And Ann said that too: it was a thread.
The men were banging the chimney about,
making it safe for winter. *Sorry,*
they said, *for all the dust.*

INTERLUDE

We walked along a sunken lane, not
much travelled, grass in the centre,
found a tree rich in yellow fruit
ripe, so took and ate, gathered more.

Then the voice of the farmer in the
field above saying *Good day*, asking
were we taking fruit.

Us, innocent, blatant, our hands behind our backs
full of soft figs, answering, *Yes.*

Take more, he says, take more, eat.

NIGHTPIECE

The mother says she saw the
                        crescent moon
and Venus, and as she walked
fireflies whizzed and burned.

So they waited. Saw the sunset's
                        fades
yellow through to flushed grey,
                        then night.

There hangs the toenail moon—
above, but nearer than, the hills—
(Venus is now a morning star).

Crickets, one nightingale in his
ancestral thicket
sings—*you, you, you, you, luck-luck, luck-
luck*—O lovely.

Stars, another glass of wine. He says,
You know I love you.

No fireflies yet. They wait.

She turns to go. *I'm tired,* and then

the darkness blinks.

POET

She died. He wrote his poem. His poem of her
and all she was. And all the how she was, (the where
the when). His poem in which he said *Oh me,*
how sad I am. Misery. Loss. Depths he
downed—for which he found apt metaphor:
Njal's burnt house; the wounded seagull on the shore.

He lived. Watched the blue mountains, the red
sky behind the far volcano. *How,* he said,
she would have loved all this. Wrote up
the sex they had: his part in her, the cups
his hands made for each heavy breast.
Bless him—the tears he flooded into words, best
he ever set in ink. And all his peers agreed;
prized his elegy, witness to the age of greed.

MIRACLE

This holy place has a large car park
also a Sunday Market—clothes, fruit,
hats, fried fish, pig (both hot and preserved).
A man with a long sharp knife
slices ham; his eyes brim up
with smiles. There's also a large church
which clangs and drones an all-day-
service.

Round the back of the church a queue,
mostly women, all older, at a door
for what must be a better class of
confession than you get at home:
deeper forgiveness, more perilous sins.
O to be washed in the blood, the blood
of the Lamb. The river tumbles past
among its grey rocks.

The best picnic spots are already
staked out, folding tables, chairs
waiting, melon, wine, water, set
to cool in the river, the last of the high
snow rushing by. Walk under the trees;
here mostly oak. A few cars have
risked the track. Find, blocked
by stones

a line to keep the cars out, this little
space, an altar rock. Behind are
two metal statues, a child kneeling,
the presence she kneels to. No

worshippers, a woman with a buggy,
river water, like an ear pulse
swoshing, swoshing—above mountain
above blue.

I stand. Notice my own brimming,
flicker in stomach and heart, brief.
I am with my family, I attend
to them, we walk. A large butterfly
orange, crosses the space, I don't know
the name, fritillary, they have such
full names, silver-washed, big.
With it, or with the naming of it, goes
the moment. Remember my knees
folded, you in a sea spray rainbow
north, north, Iona's shore? Time was
time is. Sentimental superstition
what would be God if God was, or just
the goddess of this place, the mother with the child
and the mute child who suddenly can speak.

JUDITH

The curtains closed upon her nakedness
she sleeps; brown hair spilled about her face,
the pale cover slid from her back,
arm stretched out, hand
holding the pillow's edge.

She always slept so,
the room dark, warm, the scents, tastes,
peach stone, speckled apricot
still on our tongues, lips, damp fingertips.

If I should tap the window—no—
she would not rise and barefoot step
to let me in. The curtains drawn

as if respecting death—O,
a death in the street? Her black
basque sat in a chair.

—VII—

PAX

The skin, in reverie, intensely
white, the hips narrow, shadow
in the groins, an Irish pallor,
dark cloth lifted, pulled up
over the head hair wet
from swimming, from the sudden April
drench. In the sewing box, two
rolls of elastic one white one black
needles thread scissors thimble
(what's it for? at least one thing
honestly explained) that
narrow eye of the smallest
needle. A change in the world
when you can ask a kindness
and a sharp-eyed man will do
woman's work, pushing thread
through the narrow eye
of the smallest needle and this
is not a poem about grief.

LAMMAS

When I say *they are cutting the barley*
I am speaking a dead language.
What does it signify? They: are cutting:
the barley: at most an image
out of a car window,
a machine in the corn,
as remote as (also dead) *Lammastide.*

At new year, at this new year,
a conjecture: *it is thought*
the ancestors got drunk on old beer,
ate new baked barley cake, put a boy
in a basket, cut his throat, burned him to ash—
first fruits.
Also remote (all, so).

When I say *they are cutting the barley*
I have in mind various stories,
images: a girl of ten years
holding the neck of a horse,
kissing the face of the horse; or
stooks, stacks,
threshing (further away are 'flails').

The barn has doors north and south: that way
the wind clears the chaff. The house
has a foot of chaff packed between floor
and ceiling, ceiling and roof space,
a ladder to the attic—
the hired girl slept with the apples—
this is also conjecture, a fiction.

Whoever she is, she steps out, midday
with the dark ewers of alcohol
(where are we now?) to find the men.
They are not mowers with scythes;
all they have is hooks,
sickles (sharp
the cut stubble spikes at her ankles).

You will not see her from the motorway,
she might be you, Ruth, not
sure, really, yet. While the men drink,
she picks at the skin on her wrist,
stares at a stone on the ground;
all this done much as a
snake licks at the air.

And is this so terrible? A language
invents (love, death, a journey: but my dear
the dead boy is real). Is the field
clear for the moon to rise?
The barley is cut and carted;
the women have milled
a coomb sack of it.

HOME

My sweet birdwatcher,
his lips cold from rain,
eyes aglitter with some rare bird—
like a cat hauling home a swan.

How he fills my kitchen, how dark
his layers of outdoor clothing,
how he spurts out his day story
120 miles, along the A14

then north, beyond Ipswich
the A12, how he carefully
dries his telescope, puts it away.
O who is so beautiful?

Beloved here is hot meat,
and look I have made cakes, some
little cakes with honey, with seeds,
and the tape of the football is waiting.

NIGHT AND DAY

His smile my heart   threw
open   like a white door on a great darkness,
or a lover's robe slipped
off the shoulders and fallen   and now
the morning air is full of presences—
this worn stone step, this warm oak
threshold, are radiant;
they flame like fat rose leaves, and
good ghosts dance in the silent street—
the invisible is visibly invisible;

or like how the thinnest sea mist,
though it obscures the lesser stars,
brightens, gives a glitter like tears,
presage of rain, where Venus shines,
(Verticordia, she who turns the human
heart)   so, a great
understanding seems manifest,
floods down into little words,
joy, love, and like milk spills
over—a warm plenty, a
dark door opened onto light,
his smile.

ISLAND

1.

Blue sky and blue mountains, give me
new words for the air passing
through pine trees, not sigh,
sough, sospire, an *oh* sound
held for a long breath. Midday,
the click/crack as pine cones open.

In the silences of this heat the poet
kisses his friend: it is the kiss
he did not take the last time
they were on the island. Silence
of the afternoon, silence of the trees
after the air has sped away.

The hawk with a fat lizard in its feet,
the turtle dove on the electric
wire, its purring song: at night
us saying goodbye on the lighthouse
steps, the *oh this is it* moment,
and all the stars, and the out-breath
crossing to the mainland.

2.

This is too late, and O the *when
it could have been*, years back
in the green woodland, then,
that day, *if you had kissed me then:*
and he still-stuck, not then
knowing the full-love flow went
both ways, and overflowing
saying—what? not much; not sure

how, or if, to say I *love you,*
sat together, touching heart to heart,
and not touching. Young/
old and wise, *it's too late, this.*

3.
The boat undaunted on the inner sea
island to island: love in a moment
love in a mist, love branded, scorched
shoulder flesh. There were no kisses,
the folded butterfly, black
by the window catch, stays. Shame
blunts arousal. The boat nudges
the shore, we all get out, carry
the picnic basket, cricket bats,
stroll through the tamarisks
towards the shelter of the pines,
towards the breathless pines.

MUSIC

i

Music always belongs to God; if I could sing
this is what the words would make, they would make

God, they would make a being out of this pain
and this pleasure, they would make sense and
nonsense. *This is not to be sniffed at*, I'd say.

Desperate times, desperate days, death has
had dominion, shall *not* have, though I fear
my own fallibility (mortal remains).

A simple song: rain, sea, Jerusalem,
and fishing boats. The weeks gone by
painting and mending, welding, the tractors
fixed up, engines tuned, new pennants
nailed to the markers. To be afloat on the sea
is like trumpets—so the waves tip inboard,
the engine stutters and fails, still, to be thrown
in the rise of the waves and rocked and soaked,
no wonder we do it, it is a prayer
as of the beginning of all, the lost star, ship,
and angel at the helm: we are adrift if we do not sing.

ii
A winter day. Low tide, grey mud,
the ferry waiting.
The children ran,
          clumped into the boat.

Halfway
he cut the engine.
Drifting. The last ebb.
Silence.

Then voices, children,
a wide white sky,
children, talking,
crossing the water.

ON THE A140

We should all be in love, and lost
in it, at least a dozen times—salt
to cure a soul to keep through death's
long winter, said the poet,

singing along to The Eagles,
tender of a sudden to the thought
that she had made him cuckold
however many times & lied
& lied (or 'not exactly' 'lied')
and now he did not mind.

—VIII—

MY SWEET REDHEAD

(Imitation: 'La Jolie Russe', Guillaume Apollinaire)

So, here I stand, a man of sense and feeling
knowledgeable about life and knowing
as much about death as any living
man can know. Yes, I've tried love,
its famous agonies and ecstasies:
I'm quite good at ideas—so some say—
fluent in several languages,
have knocked about the world a bit,
I've seen war as a gunner (culpable
of dishing out 'friendly' fire) and
as a foot soldier (the ones that get it
from both sides); I had a head wound—
got trepanned while under the ether—
and the war, grisly farce, slaughtered my best friends.

Let's go, you and me, put aside the war,
consider, as students of history, people
pretty well up in today's thinking,
this terminal quarrel—
tradition v creativity,
order v experiment.

You who speak for God
whose mouths are godlike
who speak for unalterable
order, please, can we beg
a little leeway? When
stood up against your saints,
your imams, your perfect
poets with their exact
hexameters, all that

manifestation of order's
perfection, forgive us
our louche insistence
on adventure, on difference.

We Are Not Your Enemies.
We can see that there are vast
blanks on the mind's maps, *Terrae
Incognitae*, jungles of desire, new
fires, colours never before seen,
a million inexplicable fantasies
to nail into the human skull.

Above all else there is the necessary
exploration of kindness, that republic
of enormous gentle silences. Above all we are stuck here
fighting on the frontiers of tomorrow,
of infinity, wrestling with time,
bending it, re-shaping it.
Can you not pity us? Can you not
wring a little compassion out of
your closed and dogmatic hearts?

Look, another violent summer comes raging in.
My young years are dead as spring in the trenches.
O sun, sun, Reason is going down in flames
but I'm still here waiting, her
passionate pilgrim watching
as she changes shape
becomes noble and gentle, enchants me,
and as I fall for her she pulls at me,
a magnet for the bullet in my heart.

Whoever your angel is, mine
is that sweet red-haired woman
with that red-gold hair
flickering like lightning
on, on, on, or flames
spreading up, peacock tails
of heat, the flare-up
of old roses just as they
blow and fade.

From: A DIARY

4 pm: Tuesday

winter evening   January

twenty-seven cranes flying north

the line of them turned
head on
dipped

they came to land hidden

the river here moving between raised banks

sunset   blood-orange red sky

in it blue darkening

> *Let us consider God's mercy:*
> *how pitiless it is.*

6.50 am: Wednesday

cars pass on the street
two sounds
engines, tyres running / the orange lamps

still guard the new houses,
keep them from night
here a robin sings trills rills
desultory chuckles
clouds / pine trees
separate from the dark

What must the wicked man do?

3.14 pm: Wednesday

there is Paine's Grey
(useful for the amateur)

but is there Goose-shit Green?

blown leaves here, oak, sweet chestnut
beech
begin to rot

     The lake surface
     how paint it? How bless
     the heart's too quick beats?

     Fear still be still.

3.36 pm: Wednesday

last year's arable is a new paddock

fenced

in it sixty-eight sheep

at the track side a man
in a black hat

picks up sticks
throws them aside

picks up sticks
throws them aside says
he is making room for the daffodils

    And again 'There is no peace,'
    says my God

    to the wicked.

2.59 pm: Thursday

in the lime tree's top winter thrushes

redwing / fieldfare / watch / take flight

thwock!

thwock!   distant
the sound of

posts being driven in

in the stubble
far off
a grey heron
hunched

wind west south west

at the pool, black water

      On the lake a long-necked grebe
      dives.

8.35 pm: Thursday

two blonde fat boys (brothers?)
tall mohican hairstyles
an
L Reg BMW parked up
at Budgens
both smoking

Shen, spirit (from the Chinese),
literally:
light in the eyes from the heart.

2.20 pm: Friday

ten dying tulips in a black jug
red black green blackthorns

flags banners pennants
brave
the standards of defeated armies

(after that battle those who lived
went into hiding—forests glens
rocky places|
some hunted down some betrayed
few survived)

the lord exultant rides his engines over all

and love wounds
is a penknife in the heart

    (It needs a sharp blade
    to cut quills.

    Try it.)